The fastest way to get ahead is to copy genius.

I0570768

***

A crumb from the winner's table is better than a feast at the losers' table.

***

We are shaped by our thoughts. We become what we think. In essence, as the saying goes, **You become what you think about most of the time.**

***

Ron A. Schaefer

"We are what we repeatedly do. Excellence, then, is not an act, but a habit."
—Will Durant, *The Story of Philosophy: The Lives and Opinions of the World's Greatest Philosophers*

In essence, **We are what we repeat.**

***

100

Handpicked
Quotes
To
Know and Grow

By Ron A. Schaefer

Ron A. Schaefer
Cover design: Getcovers.com

This book is designed to inspire and encourage personal growth through the power of thoughtful quotes. The insights shared are for general informational purposes only, with the understanding that neither the author nor the publisher is engaged in providing legal, accounting, or other professional services. If you are seeking specific guidance in areas such as legal, accounting, or financial matters, please consult a qualified professional.

A Note on Style: While I've put great care into the content of this book, I chose not to strictly follow formal grammar and style rules, like those in The Chicago Manual of Style.

Quotations are anonymous unless otherwise specified.

ISBN 979-8-9913887-0-2
Library of Congress Control Number 2024917494
First Edition Published in October 2024

Your self-talk determines your self-worth. **"***Self-talk*** is anything you repeat to yourself. It's your internal voice:**

- **Words from a song,**
- **Blogs & news,**
- **Jokes or funny stories,**
- **Negative thoughts,**
- **Mom & Dad sayings,**
- **Friends comments, or**
- **Positive self-talk from a quote book."**

—Ron A. Schaefer

***

Ron A. Schaefer

"Comments are meant to persuade."
—Ron A. Schaefer

***

"We think in pictures."
—Bob Proctor, Canadian author (1934–2022)

Essentially, **we have the ability to choose any thought we want and to build any image we wish**.

***

"Before I was paralyzed, there were 10,000 things I could do; now there are 9,000. I can either dwell on the 1,000 I've lost or focus on the 9,000 I have left."
—William Mitchell, *It's Not What Happens To You, It's What You Do About It* (1997)

Since we can **control the pictures in our mind, we can manage our thoughts.**

***

"When you think positively instead of negatively, positive results will follow. In essence, just as when you buy a new car you see the road is filled with the same car, you'll recognize more positive results."
—Ron A. Schaefer

"Only optimists win."
—Catherine Nilan; while the quote is popular, its author remains relatively obscure

"Optimism is a happiness magnet. If you stay positive, good things and good people will be drawn to you."
—Mary Lou Retton's *Gateways to Happiness: 7 Ways to a More Peaceful, More Prosperous, More Satisfying Life (2000)*

Have you ever noticed complainers love hanging out with complainers? And just the opposite is also true: **Positive people love hanging out with positive people.**

***

Ron A. Schaefer

The struggle ends when the gratitude begins.

***

"The only disability in life is a bad attitude."
—Scott Hamilton, Olympian

***

"Your best attitude is gratitude. Start by saying *Thank you*."
—Ron A. Schaefer

***

"Feedback is the breakfast of champions."
—Ken Blanchard, popularizing a saying he learned from Rick Tate

Nothing is learned from success; only from struggles.

***

"The person doing the talking wants to connect."
—Ron A. Schaefer

***

Be kind, for everyone you meet is fighting a hard battle.

***

Ron A. Schaefer

In a parable that has been circulating since at least the nineteenth century, a wise person is said to ask a gossip,

"Before you tell me, did you apply the three filters?
First, is what you're about to share true?
Second, is this information good or kind?
Third, is the information useful?"

***

"Make the most of the best and the least of the worst."
—Robert Louis Stevenson, Scottish writer and poet (1850–1894)

***

"Blaming, complaining, and explaining are all draining. Don't do it."
—James Altucher, American author and podcaster

***

"If you cannot be positive, at least be quiet."
—Joel Osteen, American pastor, televangelist

***

"Complaining is wasted time that should be used clarifying your vision."
—Ron A. Schaefer

***

"Vetted ideas lead to successful action."
—Ron A. Schaefer

***

Learn the rules like a pro so you can break them like an artist.

***

"I dream my painting and then I paint my dream."
—Vincent Van Gogh

In essence, **Clearly defined ending before beginning.**

***

Visualize before action.
1. Rehearse mentally to gain clarity in what you're about to do.
2. Greater detail will give greater chance of success.
3. Create emotional connection by talking to yourself—about what the action will look like—the body and hand movements of what you're about to do.
4. Visualize potential obstacles and how you'll get around them
5. Visualize one minute for ten minutes of action.
 —Ron A. Schaefer

***

"Which is more valuable: an idea or the execution of the idea? Only action leads to change. Two people can have the same idea, but the first to execute gets the credit."
—Ron A. Schaefer

***

Failing to plan is planning to fail.

***

Ron A. Schaefer

"Be the person you needed when you were younger."
—Ayesha Siddiqi, an author, scientist, and political commentator, in a 2013 tweet.

"While we try to teach our children all about life, our children teach us what life is all about."
—Angela Schwindt; while the quote is popular, its author remains relatively obscure

"Before having kids you can be selfish; but after having kids you become selfless."
—Ryan J. Schaefer; while the quote is popular, its author remains relatively obscure

***

The best thing you can spend on your children is your time.

"The best inheritance a parent can give to their children is a few minutes of their time each day."
—Orlando A. Battista, Canadian chemist and author (1917–1995)

"To help your children turn out well, spend twice as much time and half as much money."
—Pauline Phillips, writing as Dear Abby (1918–2013)

***

As parents, our goal is to teach our kids how to be self-reliant.

"When you know you're capable of dealing with whatever comes, you have the only security the world has to offer."
—Harry Browne, American writer and politician (1933–2006)

***

"Questions = focus."
—Ron A. Schaefer

***

Ron A. Schaefer

"Live your life in the manner that you would like your children to live theirs."
—Michael Levine, author of *Bottom Line Personal Book of Bests: Winning Words of Wisdom*

***

"Happy laughter and family voices in the home will help more kids off the streets than the strictest curfew."
—Charles Rozell Swindoll, an evangelical Christian pastor, author, educator, and radio preacher

***

"We want our children to want to develop the habit of searching for the best habits and making them their own."
—Ron A. Schaefer

***

Ron A. Schaefer

"World-renowned billionaires Warren Buffett and Bill Gates were once asked to share their secret to success in one word, and they both wrote down *focus*. According to Gates, 'The thing you do obsessively between age thirteen and eighteen, that's the thing you have the most chance of being world-class at.'"
—Charlie Rose TV interview, February 22, 2016

***

Michael Phelps, a twenty-three–time Olympic gold medalist, said on NBC's *Make It*, **"I have short-term and long-term goals."** He further emphasized that **"the short-term goals are stepping stones to my long-term goals."**

***

Similar in thought and outcome to Phelps's philosophy is this:
In his book *Breakthrough*, Scott Duffy interviewed Olympian Shaun White, who said, **"I tend to set very high goals for myself, but I also set some lower, more achievable, and playful goals. One year, my goal was to see how many cars I could win. I was around 16 years old, so driving was on my mind. Man, I won about seven cars."**

***

"When I was a boy of fourteen, my father was so ignorant I could hardly stand to have the old man around. But when I got to be twenty-one, I was astounded at how much the old man had learned in seven years."

A *Reader's Digest* anecdote, often falsely attributed to Mark Twain

***

Ron A. Schaefer

In Warren Buffet's 2013 letter to Berkshire Hathaway shareholders, he shed light on the directives he included in his will: "The cash delivered to a trustee for my wife's benefit," he wrote, **"my advice to the trustee is to put 10 percent of the cash in short-term government bonds and 90 percent in a very low-cost S&P 500 index fund."**

***

"Jeff Bezos makes his investment based on if it's going to change people's lives. Once Shaq started doing that he quadrupled his net worth."
—*Wall Street Journal* video interview, July 5, 2019

***

"Save first, and spend what's left over."
—Warren Buffett, chairperson of Berkshire Hathaway

***

"Disciplined savings = freedom."
—Ron A. Schaefer

***

"Bad debts make you a slave; good debts make you money."
—Ron A. Schaefer

***

"Would you make this purchase during a recession?"
—Ron A. Schaefer

***

"How I make a guaranteed 16 percent return? I pay off my credit card."
—Mark Cuban, American businessman and investor

***

"If we buy to make our hearts flutter, it's a want;
If we buy a trend, it's an investment;
If we buy to survive, it's a need."
—Ron A. Schaefer

***

Ron A. Schaefer

Wealth buys leisure, but not wisdom.

***

Rich people only spend interest—not principal.

***

"While my co-worker relaxes after work by watching entertaining TV shows, I invest my time in personal and professional development by watching self-improvement YouTube videos, exploring ChatGPT, and attending seminars. Who is more likely to achieve their dream?"
—Ron A. Schaefer

***

Poor people habits:
1) No annual doctor visit
2) Negative mindset—always the victim
3) Believe results are a matter of luck
4) No To-Do lists
5) No interest in learning
6) "Show me what I'm supposed to do" mentality
7) 90% of the day spent on entertainment, TV, and social media
8) Make poor choices
9) Zero money saved

—Ron A. Schaefer

***

Rich people habits:
1) **Health before wealth**
2) **Positive mindset—I control my future**
3) **Plan before planning is needed**
4) **Timed To-Do lists**
5) **Continuous learning and have libraries**
6) **"I'll figure it out" mentality**
7) **90% of day spent on searching for solutions**
8) **Network with other rich people**
9) **Multiple income streams**
10) **Give back to the community**

—Ron A. Schaefer

***

A formal education will get you a cash flow job, but to make more money you must have your own business.

"The No. 1 guideline to success is you must be in business for yourself. When you work for someone else, you sell your time at wholesale to your employer, who then re-sells it at retail to the customer."
—J. Paul Getty, American industrialist (1892–1976)

***

This thought is similar to a Zig Ziglar quote:

"If you help enough people get what they want, you'll get what you want."
—Zig Ziglar, *Treasury of Life Lessons* (1926–2012)

***

**"While driving to Costco at 6:15 a.m. for gas, normally I catch all green lights—ten of them, but this time every light was red.
I realized starting and stopping was work while all green lights was not work.
Work is getting through all the exceptions to reach your goal."**
—Ron A. Schaefer

***

Think like your customer and you will win.

***

Your customer, client, or patient "want to be treated as a friend."
—Brian Sher, In *What Rich People Know & Desperately Want to Keep Secret* (2000)

Ron A. Schaefer

When you stop treating them as a friend or family member it's time to retire.

"I will care for them as if they're my own family, and once I no longer have that mindset, I will retire…"
—Jeremy London, MD, in *How I Deal with Death as a Heart Surgeon* (YouTube, June 5, 2024)

***

"In business, convenience kills competition."
—Ron A. Schaefer

***

"If I'm moving at half speed, my goals are not clear."
—Ron A. Schaefer

***

"If everything is under control, you're going too slow."
—Mario Andretti, Italian-American former motorsports racing driver

***

"Perfection is reached, not when there is nothing left to add, but when there is nothing left to take away."
—Antoine de Saint Exupéry, French writer (1900–1944)

***

"Quality is remembered long after price is forgotten."
—Aldo Gucci, Italian designer (1905–1990)

***

Always try to do things in chronological order; it's less confusing that way.

***

You get paid for your knowledge, not your time.
Every time you learn something, that increases your value.

***

"The young man knows the rules, but the old man knows the exceptions."
—Oliver Wendell Holmes, Sr., American physician and poet (1809–1894)

***

"The young physician starts life with twenty drugs for every disease, and the old physician ends life with one drug for twenty diseases."
—William Osler, Canadian physician, (1849–1919)

***

"Your wealth is determined by your connections. Stand next to successful people."
—Ron A. Schaefer

***

"You cannot make a good deal with a bad person."
—Warren Buffett, chairperson of Berkshire Hathaway

***

"Money amplifies your personality."
—Ron A. Schaefer

***

"Run your new business ideas past potential customers to shoot holes through it. If they love it, they'll sign up."
—Mark Cuban, American businessman and investor

***

**"Losers have goals;
Winners have systems."**
—Scott Adams, creator of Dilbert

***

**"Befriend workers to get the best
work."**
—Ron A. Schaefer

***

"Humility influences people. If anything goes bad, I did it. If anything goes semi-good, we did it. If anything goes really good, then you did it."
—Bear Bryant, football player and coach (1913–1983)

***

"Ability may get you to the top, but it takes character to keep you there."
—John Wooden, American basketball coach (1910–2010)

***

"People may hear your words, but they feel your attitude."
—John C Maxwell, American author and orator

***

"Good stories always beat good spreadsheets."
—Chris Sacca, American investor

***

Ron A. Schaefer

"Great minds discuss ideas. Average minds discuss events. Small minds discuss people."
—A quote commonly attributed to Socrates (c 470–399 BCE) and rephrased by Henry Thomas Buckle, Historian and author (1821–1862)

***

"A novice can list some of the steps. A professional can list all of the steps and in the right order."
—Ron A. Schaefer

***

"You're a pro if you know what information is missing."
—Ron A. Schaefer

***

"Each problem that I solved became a rule which served afterwards to solve other problems."
—René Descartes, French philosopher and scientist (1596–1650)

***

"Time does not equal effort; persistence equals effort. Keep your thoughts on your primary task. Persistence beats resistance."
—Ron A. Schaefer

***

"Genius is perseverance in disguise."
—Mike Newlin, American basketball player

***

"Hard work beats talent when talent fails to work hard."
—Tim Nolte, high school basketball coach

***

"I find that the harder I work, the more luck I seem to have."
—Thomas Jefferson, U.S. president (1743–1846)

***

"The best business strategy is to solve the simplest, easiest, and most valuable problem."
—Reid Hoffman, American internet entrepreneur and venture capitalist

***

"I have failed more times than anyone in this room."
—Steve Harvey, American TV host

***

"Failure is a bruise not a tattoo."
—Jon Sinclair; while the quote is popular, its author remains relatively obscure

***

"To forgive is to set a prisoner free and discover that the prisoner was you."
—Lewis B. Smedes, Author (1921–2002)

In essence, **Those who do not forgive remain trapped in the prison of their own hatred.**

***

"Whatever is begun in *anger,* ends in shame."
—from *Proverbs*, collected by William Hardcastle Browne

***

 "Generally, a deal that finds you is not a deal."
—Ron A. Schaefer

***

**"Life is not about reaching and achieving retirement.
Life about pursuing excitement and happiness."**
—Sir Richard Branson, English business magnate

***

"Life is a gift. These are the most significant changes for each decade:

By age 20 we realize we're in control of our lives.

By age 30 we start to buy stuff.

By age 40 we are at our peak performance.

By age 50 we start packing retirement accounts.

By age 60 we no longer want to work overtime.

By age 70 we start having health issues.

By age 80 we stop traveling.

By age 90 we repeat the stories we remember."

—Ron A. Schaefer

***

"It's easier to cut your meals in half than to double your hours at the gym."
—Meghan T. Schaefer; while the quote is popular, its author remains relatively obscure

***

"We're attracted by appearance, we're pleased by personality, but we marry character."
—Ron A. Schaefer

***

"If you're not saying 'HELL YEAH!' about something, say no."
—Derek Sivers, *Anything You Want*

***

You can't control your history, but you can control the number of hours you put into your dream.

***

Ron A. Schaefer

"If you are still looking for that one person who will change your life, take a look in the mirror."
—Roman Price; while the quote is popular, its author remains relatively obscure

*****

The greatest project you'll ever work on is you.

*****

"Everyone writes their own life story."
—Ron A. Schaefer

*****

Thank you for taking this journey!

If you've enjoyed *100 Handpicked Quotes to Know and Grow* and want to encourage others to read it—and inspire Ron A. Schaefer to share more of his favorite quotes—please consider leaving a review on a book review website.

Your positive review is greatly appreciated!

Ron A. Schaefer

Made in the USA
San Diego, CA
1 October 2024